Simone Weil:
The Life and Times of a Radical Philosopher

Simone Weil was born on February 3, 1909, in Paris, France, to Bernard and Selma Weil. Her parents were both secular Jews of Alsatian origin. Simone was a precocious child with a keen intellect and a strong sense of empathy. Despite her secular upbringing, Simone developed a strong interest in religion and spirituality at an early age. She would later describe this as a deep longing for something she could not name.

Weil was a gifted student, excelling in her studies of philosophy at the prestigious École Normale Supérieure. Her professors recognized her talent and potential, but Weil was restless and unhappy. She felt a sense of detachment from the world around her and struggled to find meaning in her studies.

It was during this time that Weil began to explore her own spirituality. She became interested in various religious traditions and spent time studying Christian mysticism and Eastern spirituality. Her explorations led her to a deeper understanding of the interconnectedness of all things and a sense of compassion for all beings.

Weil's philosophical and spiritual interests would remain with her for the rest of her life. They would also drive her political activism and social justice work. It was during her early years at the École Normale Supérieure that Weil first began to grapple with the profound questions that would define her life's work.

The Factory Worker

Simone Weil taught briefly at a girls' school in Le Puy after her studies at École Normale Supérieure. Her life took a sharp turn when she decided to leave her comfortable academic life and work in a factory. This decision would have a profound impact on her worldview and political beliefs, and would come to define her as a committed activist and advocate for social justice.

Weil was deeply troubled by the conditions she witnessed in the factory where she worked. She saw firsthand the struggles and suffering of the workers, who were subject to long hours, low pay, and dangerous working conditions. Her experiences in the factory gave her a newfound appreciation for the dignity of labor and a deep commitment to workers' rights.

Weil's time in the factory also shaped her understanding of the relationship between power and oppression. She saw how the owners of the factory held all the power, while the workers were powerless to improve their conditions. This understanding would lead her to become a vocal opponent of fascism and totalitarianism, and a champion of democracy and individual freedom.

Her time in the factory would be a turning point in Weil's life, setting her on a new path that would lead to further political activism, philosophical exploration, and spiritual growth.

Political Activism

Weil's commitment to social justice and political activism only grew stronger in the years that followed her time in the factory. She became a leading voice in the struggle against fascism and totalitarianism, and her philosophical writings on democracy and individual freedom made her a respected figure among intellectuals and activists around the world.

Weil was deeply troubled by the rise of fascism in Europe, and she saw firsthand the devastating consequences of totalitarianism during the Spanish Civil War.

She became involved in various political and social justice movements, and her activism took her from the streets of Paris to the front lines of the Spanish conflict.

Weil's political activism was grounded in her philosophical beliefs. She believed in the fundamental dignity of all human beings, and she saw democracy as the best means of protecting individual freedom and ensuring that power was held in check. Her writings on democracy and individual freedom would go on to inspire generations of activists and intellectuals.

But Weil was not content to simply write about her beliefs. She was a tireless activist, and she worked tirelessly to promote social justice and human rights. She traveled to Spain to fight with the Republicans in the Spanish Civil War, and she worked with various resistance groups during World War II.

Weil's activism often came at a personal cost. She suffered from health problems and was frequently arrested for her political activities. But she remained steadfast in her commitment to social justice and human rights, and her writings and activism continue to inspire people around the world to this day.

Spiritual Exploration

In addition to her political activism and philosophical pursuits, Simone Weil was also deeply interested in spirituality and mystical experiences. Her search for the divine would lead her on a journey of spiritual exploration and self-discovery that would profoundly shape her later years.

Weil's interest in mysticism began in her youth, when she discovered the works of Christian mystics. As she grew older, her interest in mysticism only deepened, and she began to explore other spiritual traditions, including Hinduism and Buddhism.

Weil's mystical experiences were often intense and profound. She believed that these experiences allowed her to connect with the divine and to experience a sense of transcendence that went beyond the limitations of the material world. Her writings on mysticism would go on to influence many thinkers and writers, including the writer and philosopher Albert Camus.

Despite her interest in mysticism, Weil was never fully satisfied with any one spiritual tradition. She was a seeker, always searching for a deeper understanding of the divine and of the human condition.

The Need for Roots

Simone Weil's book "The Need for Roots" is considered one of her most important works, and it explores her ideas about community, tradition, and the importance of finding one's place in the world.

For Weil, the modern world was characterized by a profound sense of disconnection and alienation. She believed that people were cut off from their roots, and that this had led to a crisis of meaning and purpose. In "The Need for Roots," Weil argued that people needed to be connected to their communities, their traditions, and their sense of place in the world in order to live fulfilling and meaningful lives.

Weil's vision of community was deeply rooted in a sense of shared values and purpose. She believed that communities needed to be built around a common vision of the good life, and that this required a shared commitment to justice, compassion, and the common good. She was critical of individualism and consumer culture, which she believed had contributed to the breakdown of community and the erosion of shared values.

At the same time, Weil recognized that tradition could be a double-edged sword. While she believed that tradition was an important source of meaning and stability, she also recognized that tradition could be oppressive and limiting. She argued that tradition needed to be critically examined and reinterpreted in light of changing social and cultural contexts.

Ultimately, Weil's vision of the need for roots was a call to action. She believed that people needed to be actively engaged in building and strengthening their communities, and that this required a commitment to social and political change. She argued that people needed to be willing to work for the common good, even in the face of opposition and adversity.

Philosophy and Ethics

Simone Weil wrote extensively about ethics, justice, and human rights. Her philosophical ideas were closely intertwined with her political and spiritual beliefs, and they remain an important part of her legacy today.

One of Weil's central philosophical ideas was the concept of attention. For Weil, attention was not simply a matter of focusing one's mind, but rather a way of being fully present in the world.

She believed that attention was a key to understanding and responding to the suffering and injustice in the world, and that it was a necessary prerequisite for ethical action.

Weil also believed in the importance of justice and human rights. She was deeply critical of systems of power and domination, and she believed that it was the responsibility of individuals to resist injustice and work for social and political change. She believed that all human beings had a right to dignity and respect, and she worked tirelessly to promote human rights and social justice.

At the same time, Weil's philosophy was deeply informed by her spiritual beliefs. She believed that the material world was not the only reality, and that there was a transcendent dimension to existence that could be accessed through prayer, meditation, and contemplation. She believed that the pursuit of spiritual truth was intimately connected to the pursuit of social and political justice.

Legacy

As World War II approached, Weil became increasingly involved in anti-fascist activities. In 1942, Weil fled from Nazi-occupied

France to London and worked briefly for the French Resistance. However, her health was already in decline, and she contracted tuberculosis shortly after arriving in England. Despite her illness, she continued to work and write until her death on August 24, 1943, at the young age of 34.

Despite living only a brief and often painful life, Simone Weil's ideas continue to have a profound impact on contemporary thought. Her unique combination of philosophy, activism, and spirituality has inspired countless individuals across a wide range of fields.

Simone Weil's legacy is a testament to the power of ideas and the enduring impact of a life well-lived. Her ideas and example continue to inspire and challenge us today, and they serve as a reminder that even in the darkest of times, there is always hope for a better world. Her words are often characterized by their depth, clarity, and uncompromising commitment to truth. Her quotations can be both illuminating and challenging, encouraging us to rethink our assumptions about the world and our place in it.

Stars and blossoming
fruit-trees: utter
permanence and
extreme fragility
give an equal sense
of eternity.

Do not allow yourself
to be imprisoned by
any affection. Keep
your solitude. The
day, if it ever comes,
when you are given
true affection, there
will be no opposition
between interior
solitude and
friendship, quite the
reverse. It is even by
this infallible sign
that you will
recognize it.

In war, an army is not
a collection of souls,
but of living,
breathing bodies.
A man thinks he is
dying for his country,
but he is dying for a
few industrialists.

Imaginary evil is romantic and varied; real evil is gloomy, monotonous, barren, boring. Imaginary good is boring; real good is always new, marvelous, intoxicating.

We do not obtain the
most precious gifts by
going in search of them
but by waiting for them.
Man cannot discover
them by his own powers,
and if he sets out to
seek for them he will
find in their place
counterfeits of which
he will be unable to
discern falsity.

The instruments of
power — arms, gold,
machines, magical or
technical secrets —
always exist
independently of him
who disposes of them,
and can be taken up by
others. Consequently
all power is unstable.

The man who has known
pure joy, if only for a
moment... is the only man
for whom affliction is
something devastating.
At the same time he is the
only man who has not
deserved the punishment.
But, after all, for him it
is no punishment; it is God
holding his hand and
pressing rather hard.
For, if he remains
constant, what he will
discover buried deep
under the sound of his own
lamentations is the pearl
of the silence of God.

Every being cries
out in silence to be
read differently. Do
not be indifferent
to these cries.

Nothing is worse
than extreme
affliction which
destroys the "I" from
the outside, because
after that we can no
longer destroy it
ourselves.

Purity is the power
to contemplate
defilement.

Our patriotism comes straight from the Romans...The Romans really were an atheistic and idolatrous people; not idolatrous with regard to images made of stone or bronze, but idolatrous with regard to themselves. It is this idolatry of self which they have bequeathed to us in the form of patriotism.

The collective is the
object of all idolatry,
this it is which chains
us to the earth. In the
case of avarice: gold is
of the social order.
In the case of ambition:
power is of the social
order. Science and art
are full of the social
element also. And love?
Love is more or less of
an exception: that is
why we can go to God
through love, not
through avarice
and ambition.

At the very best, a mind enclosed in language is in prison. It is limited to the number of relations which words can make simultaneously present to it; and remains in ignorance of thoughts which involve the combination of a greater number...So the mind moves in a closed space of partial truth, which may be larger or smaller, without ever being able so much as to glance at what is outside.

The danger is not lest
the soul should doubt
whether there is any
bread, but lest, by a
lie, it should persuade
itself that it is not
hungry.

The great error of nearly all studies of war, an error into which all socialists have fallen, has been to consider war as an episode in foreign politics when it is especially an act of internal politics and the most atrocious act of all ... Since the directing apparatus has no other way of fighting the enemy than by sending its own soldiers, under compulsion, to their death-the war of one state against another state resolves itself into a war of the state and the military apparatus against its own people.

One has only the
choice between God
and idolatry. There is
no other possibility.
For the faculty of
worship is in us, and
it is either directed
somewhere into this
world, or into
another.

Attention is the
rarest and purest
form of generosity.

Grace fills empty
spaces, but it can
only enter where
there is a void to
receive it, and it is
grace itself which
makes this void.

The vulnerability of
precious things is
beautiful because
vulnerability is a
mark of existence.
The destruction of
Troy. The fall of the
petals from fruit
trees in blossom.
To know that what is
most precious is not
rooted in existence -
that is beautiful.

There is something
else which has the
power to awaken us to
the truth. It is the
works of writers of
genius. They give us,
in the guise of
fiction, something
equivalent to the
actual density of the
real, that density
which life offers us
every day but which we
are unable to grasp
because we are amusing
ourselves with lies.

A hurtful act is the transference to others of the degradation which we bear in ourselves.

Attachment is the
great fabricator of
illusions; reality
can be attained only
by someone who is
detached.

Whether the mask is labeled fascism, democracy, or dictatorship of the proletariat, our great adversary remains the apparatus—the bureaucracy, the police, the military. Not the one facing us across the frontier of the battle lines, which is not so much our enemy as our brothers' enemy, but the one that calls itself our protector and makes us its slaves. No matter what the circumstances, the worst betrayal will always be to subordinate ourselves to this apparatus and to trample underfoot, in its service, all human values in ourselves and in others.

Those who are
unhappy have no need
for anything in this
world but people
capable of giving
them their
attention.

The destruction of
the past is perhaps
the greatest of all
crimes.

A doctrine serves no
purpose in itself, but
it is indispensable
to have one if only to
avoid being deceived
by false doctrines.

During the last quarter of a century all the authority associated with the function of spiritual guidance ... has seeped down into the lowest publications. ... Between a poem by Valéry and an advertisement for a beauty cream promising a rich marriage to anyone who used it there was at no point a breach of continuity. So as a result of literature's spiritual usurpation a beauty cream advertisement possessed, in the eyes of little village girls, the authority that was formerly attached to the words of priests.

The needs of a human
being are sacred. Their
satisfaction cannot be
subordinated either to
reasons of state, or to
any consideration of
money, nationality,
race, or color, or to the
moral or other value
attributed to the human
being in question, or to
any consideration
whatsoever.

There is one, and only
one, thing in modern
society more hideous
than crime namely,
repressive justice.

We are like plants
which have the one
choice of being in or
out of the light.

At the centre of the
human heart is the
longing for an
absolute good, a
longing which is
always there and is
never appeased by any
object in this world.

We possess nothing in
the world — a mere
chance can strip us of
everything — except
the power to say 'I'.

Absolutely unmixed
attention is prayer.

Even if our efforts
of attention seem for
years to be producing
no result, one day a
light that is in exact
proportion to them
will flood the soul.

If a captive mind is unaware of being in prison, it is living in error. If it has recognized the fact, even for the tenth of a second, and then quickly forgotten it in order to avoid suffering, it is living in falsehood. Men of the most brilliant intelligence can be born, live and die in error and falsehood. In them, intelligence is neither a good, nor even an asset. The difference between more or less intelligent men is like the difference between criminals condemned to life imprisonment in smaller or larger cells. The intelligent man who is proud of his intelligence is like a condemned man who is proud of his large cell.

Official history is a matter of believing murderers on their own word.

If you say to someone who has ears to hear: "What you are doing to me is not just," you may touch and awaken at its source the spirit of attention and love. But it is not the same with words like, "I have the right..." or "you have no right to..." They evoke a latent war and awaken the spirit of contention.

Difficult as it is
really to listen to
someone in affliction,
it is just as difficult
for him to know that
compassion is
listening to him.

The glossy surface
of our civilization
hides a real
intellectual
decadence.

Power ... is the
supreme end for all
those who have not
understood.

Two prisoners
whose cells adjoin
communicate with each
other by knocking on
the wall. The wall
is the thing which
separates them but is
also their means of
communication. It is
the same with us and
God. Every separation
is a link.

Evil when we are in
its power is not
felt as evil but as
a necessity, or
even a duty.

A beautiful woman
looking at her image
in the mirror may very
well believe the image
is herself. An ugly
woman knows it is not.

Love of God is
pure when joy and
suffering inspire
an equal degree of
gratitude.

Real genius is
nothing else but the
supernatural virtue
of humility in the
domain of thought.

The authentic and pure
values, truth, beauty, and
goodness, in the activity of
a human being are the result
of one and the same act,
a certain application of the
full attention to the object.
Teaching should have no aim
but to prepare, by training
the attention, for the
possibility of such an act.
All the other advantages of
instruction are without
interest.

To die for God is not a proof of faith in God. To die for an unknown and repulsive convict who is a victim of injustice, that is a proof of faith in God.

At the bottom of the heart
of every human being,
from earliest infancy
until the tomb, there is
something that goes on
indomitably expecting,
in the teeth of all
experience of crimes
committed, suffered, and
witnessed, that good and
not evil will be done to
him. It is this above all
that is sacred in every
human being.

Art is the symbol of
the two noblest human
efforts: to construct
and to refrain from
destruction.

Just as a person who is always asserting that he is too good-natured is the very one from whom to expect, on some occasion, the coldest and most unconcerned cruelty, so when any group sees itself as the bearer of civilization this very belief will betray it into behaving barbarously at the first opportunity.

The sea is not less
beautiful in our eyes
because we know that
sometimes ships are
wrecked by it.

We only possess what
we renounce; what we
do not renounce
escapes from us.

Although it is beyond the reach of any human faculties, man has the power of turning his attention and love towards it. Nothing can ever justify the assumption that any man, whoever he may be, has been deprived of this power. It is a power which is only real in this world in so far as it is exercised. The sole condition for exercising it is consent.

Every sin is an
attempt to fly from
emptiness.

We have to try to
cure our faults by
attention and not
by will.

When a man's life is destroyed or damaged by some wound or privation of soul or body, which is due to other men's actions or negligence, it is not only his sensibility that suffers but also his aspiration toward the good. Therefore there has been sacrilege towards that which is sacred in him.

To be rooted is perhaps the most important and least recognized need of the human soul... A human being has roots by virtue of his real, active and natural participation in the life of a community which preserves in living shape certain particular treasures of the past and certain particular expectations for the future. This participation is a natural one, in the sense that it is automatically brought about by place, conditions of birth, profession and social surroundings. Every human being needs to have multiple roots. It is necessary for him to draw wellnigh the whole of his moral, intellectual and spiritual life by way of the environment of which he forms a natural part.

Whenever one tries to
suppress doubt ,
there is tyranny .

It is an eternal
obligation toward
the human being not
to let him suffer from
hunger when one has a
chance of coming to
his assistance.

The work of art which
I do not make, none
other will ever make.

Truth is sought not
because it is truth
but because it is
good.

He who does not realize to
what extent shifting fortune
and necessity hold in
subjection every human
spirit, cannot regard as
fellow-creatures nor love
as he loves himself those
whom chance separated from
him by an abyss. The variety
of constraints pressing upon
man give rise to the illusion
of several distinct species
that cannot communicate.
Only he who has measured the
dominion of force, and knows
how not to respect it, is
capable of love and justice.

School children and students who love God should never say: "For my part I like mathematics"; "I like French"; "I like Greek." They should learn to like all these subjects, because all of them develop that faculty of attention which, directed toward God, is the very substance of prayer.

The only way into
truth is through one's
own annihilation;
through dwelling a
long time in a state of
extreme and total
humiliation.

I also am other than
what I imagine myself
to be. To know this is
forgiveness.

Workers need poetry
more than bread.
They need that their
life should be a poem.
They need some light
from eternity.

Human beings are so
made that the ones who
do the crushing feel
nothing; it is the
person crushed who
feels what is happening.
Unless one has placed
oneself on the side of
the oppressed, to feel
with them, one cannot
understand.

Equality is the public recognition, effectively expressed in institutions and manners, of the principle that an equal degree of attention is due to the needs of all human beings. Hierarchy is the scale of responsibilities. Since attention is inclined to direct itself upwards and remain fixed, special provisions are necessary to ensure the effective compatibility of equality and hierarchy.

The recognition of human
wretchedness is difficult
for whoever is rich and
powerful because he is
almost invincibly led
to believe that he is
something. It is equally
difficult for the man in
miserable circumstances
because he is almost
invincibly led to
believe that the rich
and powerful man
is something.

It is much easier to
imagine ourselves in
the place of God the
Creator than in the
place of Christ
crucified.

The love of our
neighbor in all its
fullness simply means
being able to say,
"What are you going
through?"

The right to kill:
supposing the life of
X ... were linked with
our own so that the
two deaths had to be
simultaneous, should
we still wish him to
die? If with our whole
body and soul we
desire life and if
nevertheless without
lying, we can reply
'yes', then we have the
right to kill.

What a country calls
its vital economic
interests are not the
things which enable
its citizens to live,
but the things which
enable it to make war.
Petrol is more likely
than wheat to be a
cause of international
conflict.

Humanism was not wrong in thinking that truth, beauty, liberty, and equality are of infinite value, but in thinking that man can get them for himself without grace.

Justice consists in seeing that no harm is done to men. Whenever a man cries inwardly: 'Why am I being hurt?' harm is being done to him. He is often mistaken when he tries to define the harm, and why and by whom it is being inflicted on him. But the cry itself is infallible.

The children of God
should not have any
other country here below
but the universe itself,
with the totality of all
the reasoning creatures
it ever has contained,
contains, or ever will
contain. That is the
native city to which
we owe our love.

God's love for us is
not the reason for
which we should love
him. God's love for us
is the reason for us
to love ourselves.

Modern life is given
over to immoderation.
Immoderation invades
everything: actions
and thought, public
and private life.

The feeding of
those that are
hungry is a form
of contemplation.

Prayer consists
simply in giving to
God all the careful
attention of which
the soul is capable.

The joy of learning is as indispensable in study as breathing is in running.

To anyone who does
actually consent to
directing his attention
and love beyond the world,
towards the reality that
exists outside the reach of
all human faculties, it is
given to succeed in doing
so. In that case, sooner or
later, there descends upon
him a part of the good,
which shines through him
upon all that surrounds
him.

When war is waged, it is for
the purpose of safeguarding
or increasing one's capacity
to make war. International
politics are wholly involved
in this vicious cycle. What
is called national prestige
consists in behaving always
in such a way as to demoralize
other nations by giving them
the impression that, if it
comes to war, one would
certainly defeat them. What is
called national security is
an imaginary state of affairs
in which one would retain the
capacity to make war while
depriving all other countries
of it.

We must love all
facts, not for their
consequences, but
because in each fact
God is there present.

One of the most exquisite
pleasures of human love
— to serve the loved one
without his knowing it
— is only possible, as
regards the love of God,
through atheism.

When an apprentice gets hurt, or complains of being tired, the workmen and peasants have this fine expression: "It is the trade entering his body." Each time that we have some pain to go through, we can say to ourselves quite truly that it is the universe, the order and beauty of the world, and the obedience of God that are entering our body.

Love: To feel with
one's whole self
the existence of
another being.

When once a certain class
of people has been placed
by the temporal and
spiritual authorities
outside the ranks of
those whose life has
value, then nothing
comes more naturally
to men than murder.

Everything without
exception which is of
value in me comes from
somewhere other than
myself, not as a gift but
as a loan which must be
ceaselessly renewed.

Justice, truth, and
beauty are sisters
and comrades. With
three such beautiful
words we have no need
to look for any
others.

The afflicted are not
listened to. They are
like someone whose
tongue has been cut out
and who occasionally
forgets the fact. When
they move their lips no
ear perceives any sound.
And they themselves soon
sink into impotence in
the use of language,
because of the certainty
of not being heard.

Everything which originates from pure love is lit with the radiance of beauty.

There is no greater joy
for me than looking at
the sky on a clear night
with an attention so
concentrated that all
my other thoughts
disappear; then one can
think that the stars
enter into one's soul.

To desire friendship
is a great fault.
Friendship should be a
gratuitous joy like
those afforded by art
or life. We must refuse
it so that we may be
worthy to receive it;
it is of the order of
grace.

It is a fault to wish
to be understood
before we have made
ourselves clear to
ourselves.

Bourgeois society is infected by monomania: the monomania of accounting. For it, the only thing that has value is what can be counted in francs and centimes. It never hesitates to sacrifice human life to figures which look well on paper, such as national budgets or industrial balance sheets.

Imagination and
fiction make up more
than three quarters
of our real life.

Everybody knows that really intimate conversation is only possible between two or three. As soon as there are six or seven, collective language begins to dominate.
That is why it is a complete misinterpretation to apply to the Church the words 'Wheresoever two or three are gathered together in my name, there am I in the midst of them.' Christ did not say two hundred, or fifty, or ten. He said two or three.